GALVELMORE HOUSE
5 GALVELMORE STREET
CRIEFF
PERTHSHIRE
PH7 4BY

D1338507

HOFFNUNG'S LITTLE ONES

By the author of:
THE MAESTRO
THE HOFFNUNG SYMPHONY ORCHESTRA
THE HOFFNUNG MUSIC FESTIVAL
THE HOFFNUNG COMPANION TO MUSIC
HOFFNUNG'S MUSICAL CHAIRS
HOFFNUNG'S ACOUSTICS
HOFFNUNG'S HUMORESQUE
HOFFNUNG IN HARMONY
HOFFNUNG'S BOOKWORMS

Hoffnung's
LITTLE ONES

SOUVENIR PRESS

© 1961 by Annetta Hoffnung

First published 1961
by Dennis Dobson

This edition first published 1988
by Souvenir Press Ltd
43 Great Russell Street, London WC1B 3PA
and simultaneously in Canada

All Rights Reserved. No part of this publication
may be reproduced, stored in a retrieval system,
or transmitted, in any form or by any means, electronic,
mechanical, photocopying, recording or otherwise
without the prior permission of the Copyright owner

ISBN 0 285 62871 2

Printed and bound in Great Britain by
William Clowes Limited, Beccles and London

Am I like papa.....   ... or Mama...

... or Uncle Horatio....

... or Great-
Aunt Phoebe

Or ...

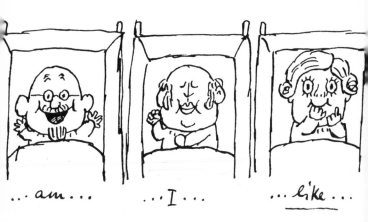

... am ...   ... I ...   ... like ...

..some...   ....body... ..else .

Or am I

like me?

A Recital (continuoso).

There, there, there . . . . . (etc.)

A complete Mystery.

On the morrow.

Mistakes
are liable to
be made.

" Matilda told such dreadful lies,
it made one gasp and stretch one's eyes. "

Playing 'Motorbyke' with Grandpa

pressing the right button

Goodnight !